FOREWORD

QE2 HAS A CLOSE AFFINITY WITH LIVERPOOL – AS DOES CUNARD ITSELF.

QE2 was planned and designed in the Cunard Building on the Pier Head, while Queen Mary and Queen Elizabeth were both registered in Liverpool, although sadly they were too big to be able to visit.

QE2, of course, has visited many times - this is the eighth – and the welcome the city gave her the first time in 1990 on the occasion of Cunard's 150th anniversary, when over a million people turned out, is the stuff of legend.

Cunard was born in Liverpool, and the company's progress to one of the great businesses of the world was achieved here. The firm was established here in 1839 at premises in Water Street, and in 1916 moved into its magnificent purpose-built Head office at the Pier Head where so much Cunard history was forged.

In Liverpool, Cunard developed from being a small and rather insignificant company with just four ships, to being one of the biggest shipping companies in the world. A huge and complex empire was run from this city.

Cunard may have physically left Liverpool, but our heart remains here. We started here and we developed here. I hope this visit by QE2, the most famous ship afloat, on the occasion of her 40th anniversary, exemplifies how much Liverpool means to Cunard.

Carol Marlow

President and Managing Director, Cunard Line

INTRODUCTION

QUEEN ELIZABETH 2 has always been a crowd-puller. Time and time again in every port of call around the world people turn out in all weathers, at all times of the day and night to see one of the world's greatest icons.

High on the list of most memorable arrivals in this great ship's 40 years at sea is Liverpool.

It's more than 17 years since QE2 first made her way up the Mersey during her maiden call at Cunard Line's spiritual home.

Those who witnessed that memorable visit joined a worldwide fan club of the most famous ocean liner in the world.

For her part, QE2 has gone to war as a troop ship, hosted Royalty and witnessed world events unfold. In doing so she has secured her own place in history.

Today, in port, has been like every other day in port in these last 40 years.
Crowds have gathered at dock gates and fences; staring, gazing and wondering.

Now, the last voyages beckon the great ocean liner towards retirement.

To help celebrate this remarkable ship's close associations with Liverpool, as well as her unique place in maritime history, it has been a privilege to look back through archives and interview a former Commodore and a former Captain.

This special commemorative publication is by no means an exhaustive history of a great ship. But for anyone who has stood on a quayside or a riverbank or a beach and looked in awe at this great Cunarder alongside or passing by, it is an insight into what makes her so very special in the hearts and minds of people all over the world.

TONY STOREY
Port of Gibraltar, June 7, 2007

1964

BUILD AND LAUNCH

BY THE LATE 1950S, Cunard Line started to ponder how best to replace the Queen Mary and the Queen Elizabeth.

The original plan had been to build two new liners with financial help from Government subsidies.

A special committee was set up under the leadership of Lord Chandos to consider the best way forward.

At the time, there was considerable doubt over the viability of a new generation of transatlantic liner entering service.

THIS WAS THE DAWN OF THE JET AGE when a crossing of the Atlantic between Europe and North America could be achieved in a matter of hours, not days.

Who would want to spend so much time getting from one side to the other by ship when they could fly?, asked the doubters.

Cunard itself realised the threat posed by air travel and, after buying British Eagle Airways in 1959, ran foul of regulations designed to safeguard the British Overseas Airways Corporation's business. Eventually, BOAC and Cunard Line reached a trading agreement to operate the principal British air service on the North Atlantic.

By the mid 1960's Cunard Line executives realised they did not have sufficient resource to purchase new aircraft as well as new tonnage, and a deal was struck allowing BOAC to buy Cunard's share of their joint operations for £11.5m.

After long and protracted debates and discussions over whether the Government of the day should subsidise the building of a new liner for Cunard, in the summer of 1963 a plan for the construction of what was to become QE2 was approved by the Government – together with a loan of more than £17m.

The contract to build the new liner was signed between Cunard Line and John Brown (Clydebank) Limited on 30th December 1964.

1967

That marked a momentous milestone – and prompted a flurry of activity at Cunard's Pier Head headquarters in Liverpool.

Teams of designers and engineers from the Glasgow yard worked tirelessly with Cunard's own Liverpool-based experts poring over every detail of the new liner's design. Designers and architects worked at their drawing boards in Liverpool's famous Cunard Building preparing every detail of the new liner. After the signing of the contract between Cunard and the ship's builders John Brown in 1964, work at the Line's Pier Head headquarters intensified under the direction of Cunard's naval architect Dan Wallace.

To this day, the efforts of the design team based at Pier Head are recorded on a plaque set into the former Board Room table at Cunard Building.

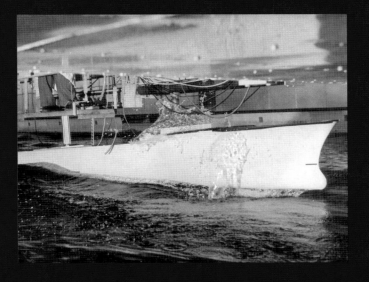

Today, more than 40 years on, their meticulous attention to detail and design is still evident on the most famous liner in the world.

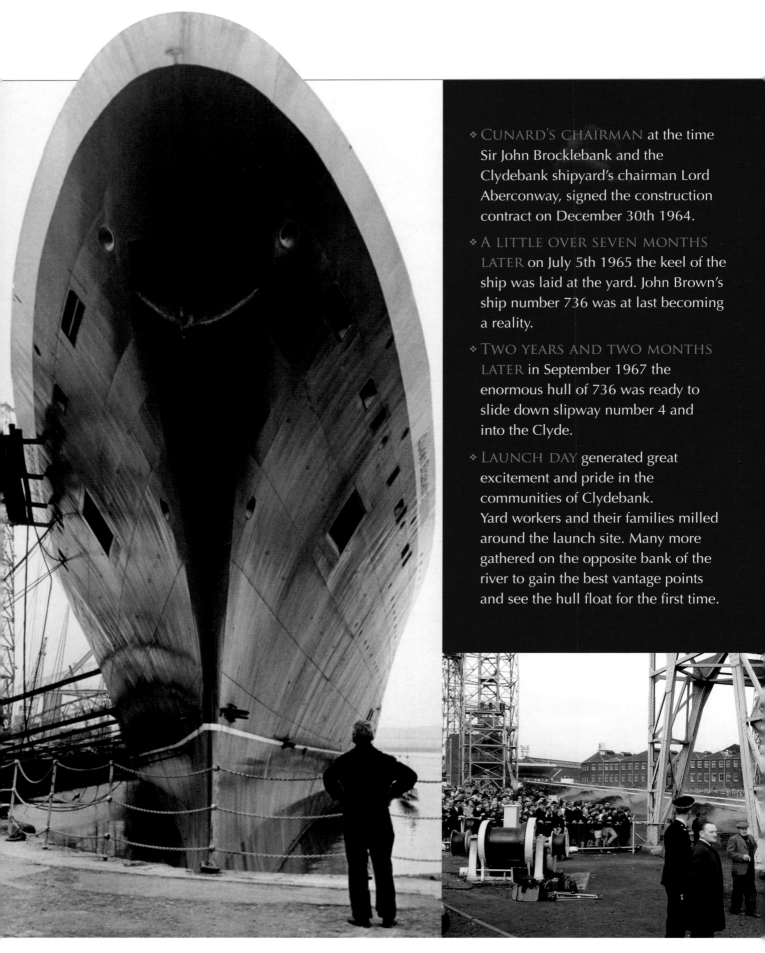

❖ CUNARD'S CHAIRMAN at the time
Sir John Brocklebank and the
Clydebank shipyard's chairman Lord
Aberconway, signed the construction
contract on December 30th 1964.

❖ A LITTLE OVER SEVEN MONTHS
LATER on July 5th 1965 the keel of the
ship was laid at the yard. John Brown's
ship number 736 was at last becoming
a reality.

❖ TWO YEARS AND TWO MONTHS
LATER in September 1967 the
enormous hull of 736 was ready to
slide down slipway number 4 and
into the Clyde.

❖ LAUNCH DAY generated great
excitement and pride in the
communities of Clydebank.
Yard workers and their families milled
around the launch site. Many more
gathered on the opposite bank of the
river to gain the best vantage points
and see the hull float for the first time.

1967

After her successful launch,
QE2 remained at the
shipyard for fitting out

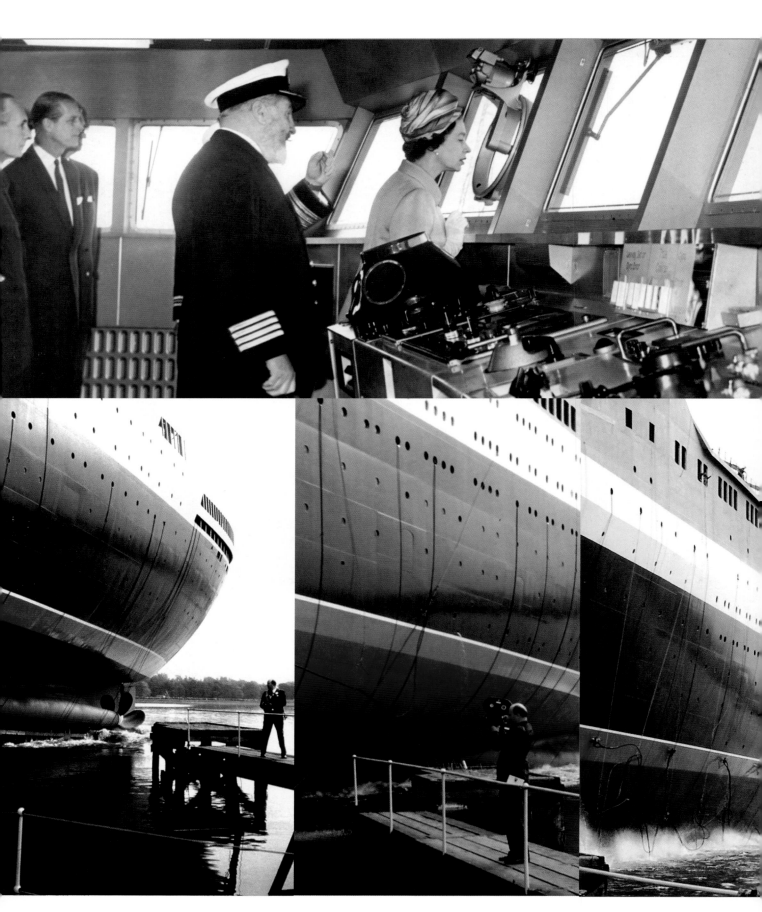

1967

❖ HER MAJESTY QUEEN ELIZABETH II
had consented to name the new liner and
in the weeks before the launch day
speculation about its name was rife.
At that stage the ship was known only
as order number 736.

❖ THE ROYAL PARTY climbed to the
launching platform and, continuing the
traditions of the launching ceremony,
the Queen was handed an envelope
containing a slip of paper on which the
proposed name of the new liner had
been written.

Cunard's lion rampant
emblem remains above the
door of Cunard Building

A written reminder of the ship's name was considered essential after one VIP reportedly forgot the name of the vessel over which they had been invited to officiate.

A similar envelope to the one on the Clydebank launch platform was resting in the safe at Cunard's New York office in case of some slip up on this side of the Atlantic.

The Queen declined the envelope, reportedly joking: "I won't be needing that!" Seconds later, at the microphone and speaking in a clear and confident voice, Her Majesty said:

"I name this ship Queen Elizabeth the Second. May God bless her and all who sail in her."

The Queen then used a pair of gold scissors to cut a ribbon releasing a bottle of Australian white wine against the hull of the Liner. These were the same scissors that her mother and grandmother had previously used at ceremonies to launch their namesake vessels.

Queen El

1967

The envelope that she had declined to accept – and the one in New York – had contained the name Queen Elizabeth.

After the launch, Cunard's then Chairman Sir Basil Smallpiece consulted with royal aides and it was agreed that the suffix "Second" would be written as the Arabic "2" and not the Roman "II".

This was considered a sensible move for a variety of reasons. At the time only battleships had carried a reigning monarch's Roman numeral suffix, and the Queen was, in fact only Queen Elizabeth I of Scotland – thus to name the ship with "II" could have offended the people of the country which had produced the hull of the new liner and, critically for Cunard, who were still required to fit her out for service.

Forty years on, Queen Elizabeth 2 has become the most famous ship in the world – as well as the one whose name is so often misprinted.

beth 2

THE MIGHTY AND MAJESTIC LINER COMES TO LIFE...

1967

FLOATING INTO THE CLYDE AT 2.28PM ON SEPTEMBER 20, 1967

EARLY INTERIOR

IN HER EARLY DAYS AT SEA, QE2 epitomised the design sophistication of the late 1960s. Her public rooms (below and right) were furnished to the highest standards of the day. In their cabins (bottom), guests enjoyed all modern conveniences – including air conditioning.

QE2 interior decor and design featured in a special exhibition at London's Design Centre, which included a mock up table setting from the Britannia Restaurant. Cabins were spacious and comfortable (right), while the Princess Grill (opposite, top right) remains one of the most unaltered rooms on the ship after 40 years

STARS ABOARD

Ever since Prince Charles became her first passenger, QE2 has hosted more famous faces than any other ship in service.

Famous faces have long crossed the oceans on board Cunard liners – and QE2 has welcomed on board many of the world's best known heads of state, politicians, sports and screen stars, church leaders and celebrities.

In the 1920s and 1930s, QE2's illustrious sisters put the golden age of steam travel firmly on the map, reminding guests that "getting there is half the fun."

Travellers from all walks of life including Royalty and celebrities were indulged with Cunard Line's famous White Star Service.

After entering service in the late, swinging sixties, and despite the growing popularity of jet flight, QE2 soon established herself as the preferred form of transatlantic travel for the stars of the day.

Her famous passengers

MEMBERS OF ROYAL FAMILIES AND THE ARISTOCRACY
HM The Queen, HRH The Duke of Edinburgh, HRH The Prince of Wales, HRH The Prince Edward, Diana, Princess of Wales, King Hussein of Jordan, The Emperor of Japan, Princess Christine of the Netherlands, Prince Nikita Romanoff, The Sultan of Brunei, The Sultan of Selanghor, The Saudi Royal Family, Earl Mountbatten, Earl of Snowdon, Earl of Lichfield, Lord Wedgwood, Lord Montagu of Beaulieu

POLITICIANS, DIPLOMATS AND CHURCHMEN WHO HAVE TRAVELLED:
Lord Archer of Weston-super-Mare, George Bush Jnr, President Jimmy Carter, Edwina Currie, Sir Nicholas Fairbairn, H R Haldeman, Bob Hawke, Sir Rex Hunt, Dame Jill Knight, Mayor John Lindsay, Lee Kuan Yew, Graca Machel, President Nelson Mandela, Lord Mason of Barnsley, Shimon Peres, Dame Stella Rimington, The Most Revd Lord Runcie of Cuddesdon, Sir Cyril Smith, Lord Taylor of Warwick

MUSICIANS
Moira Anderson, Applejacks, Larry Adler, Charles Aznavour, Count Basie, Dave Berry, John Briggs, Joe Brown, The Cure, Vic Damone, Gracie Fields, Wayne Fontana, Gerry and the Pacemakers, Marvin Hamlisch, George Harrison, Herman's Hermits, Edmund Hockridge, Mick Jagger, Elton John, Davy Jones, Jack Jones, Frankie Laine, Joe Loss, Patti Lupone, Dame Vera Lynn, Maureen McGovern, Harry Neilson, Yoko Ono, Oscar Peterson, Linda Ronstadt, Neil Sedaka, Carly Simon, Ringo Starr, Rod Stewart, Tommy Tune, Frankie Vaughan, Sarah Vaughan, Nancy Wilson

EMINENT JOURNALISTS AND AUTHORS
Fiona Armstrong, Beryl Bainbridge, Lynne Barber, Alan Bleasdale, Carol Barnes, Jennie Bond, Craig Brown, Michael Brunson, Michael Buerk, Paul Burrell, Bill Bryson, Tom Clancy, Matthew Collins, Clive Cussler, Frank Delaney,

Queen Elizabeth II and Prince Philip, Prince Charles, Nelson Mandela, Elton John, Beryl Bainbridge and Bill Bryson

Peter Sissons, Thelma Barlow, Prunella Scales, Jack Charlton, Murray Walker and Millvina Dean

Colin Dexter, Dick Francis, Sandy Gall, Tim Heald, Hannah Hauxwell, Richard Hendrick, Brian Hitchen, Mary Higgins Clark, Sir Bernard Ingham, Virginia Ironside, Paul Johnson, P D James, Sir Ludovic Kennedy, Roddy Llewellyn, Jackie and Sunny Mann, Brian Masters, Frank McCourt, Angus McGill, James Mitchener, Sheridan Morley, Flt Lt John Nichol, Sir David Nicholas, Pat O'Brien, Anna Pavard, Marje Proops, Claire Rayner, Celia Sandys, Selina Scott, Michael Shea, Mary Ann Sieghart, John Simpson, Peter Sissons, Sir Roy Strong, Carol Thatcher, Leslie Thomas, Jack Tinker, Hugo Vickers, Terry Waite, Tony Warren, Tennessee Williams, Nigel West, Roland White

STARS OF STAGE AND SCREEN INCLUDING

John Altman, Eamonn Andrews, Julie Andrews, Michael Aspel, Peter Baldwin, Roy Barraclough, Thelma Barlow, Jeremy Beadle, Sean Bean, Isla Blair, Victor Borge, Jim Bowen, George Burns, Richard Burton, James Cagney, Jasper Carrott, Judith Chalmers, Petula Clark, Glenn Close, Rosemary Conley, Bill Cosby, Judy Cornwell, Michael Crawford, Jimmy Cricket, Tim Curry, Tony Curtis, Jill Dando, Paul Daniels, Nigel Davenport, Les Dawson, Dame Judi Dench, Neil Diamond, Douglas Fairbanks Jnr, Bryan Forbes, Fiona Fullerton, Lillian Gish, Jilly Goolden, Russell Grant, Richard Griffiths, Larry Hagman, Stuart Hall, Rolf Harris, Dickie Henderson, Jim Henson, Sherrie Hewson, Thora Hird, Bob Holness, Bob Hope, Frankie Howerd, Rock Hudson, Lorraine Kelly, Eric Knowles, Robert Kilroy Silk, Kris Kristofferson, Burt Lancaster, Danny LaRue, Christopher Lee, Maureen Lipman, Barry Manilow, Dean Martin, Raymond Massey, Hayley Mills, Sir John Mills, Matthew Modine, Bob Monkhouse, Nannette Newman, Paul Newman, Barry Norman, Tom O'Connor, Sid Owen, Patsy Palmer, Nicholas Parsons, John Peal, Robert Powell, Vincent Price, Esther Rantzen, Lyn Redgrave, Christopher Reeve, Debbie Reynolds, Gary Rhodes, Wendy Richards, Angela Rippon, Ginger Rogers, Anton Rodgers, Patricia Routledge, Dr Ruth, Sir Sydney Samuelson, Telly Savalas, Sir Jimmy Savile, Prunella Scales, George C Scott, Sir Harry Secombe, Peter Sellers, Delia Smith, Jon Snow, Terence Stamp, Tommy Steele, Sharon Stone, Meryl Streep, Jimmy Tarbuck, Chris Tarrant, Elizabeth Taylor, James Taylor, Christopher Timothy, Anthony Worral Thompson, John Travolta, Twiggy, Sir Peter Ustinov, Bill Waddington, Robert Wagner, Barbara Windsor, Alan Whicker, Richard Whitley, Desmond Wilcox, Ernie Wise, Helen Worth, Timothy West, Michael York

SPORTS PERSONALITIES

Eric Bristow, Frank Bruno, Sir Matt Busby, Jack Charlton, Sir Colin Cowdry, Brian Close, Kenny Dalglish, Steve Davis, Keith Deller, Alan Hansen, Stephen Hendry, Denis Law, Cliff Lazarenko, David Platt, Tessa Sanderson, Nobby Stiles, Daley Thompson, Murray Walker

EXPLORERS

Colonel John Blashford-Snell, Sir Chris Bonington, Jean-Michel Cousteau, John Harrison, Sir Wally Herbert, Brian Jones, Dr Kathryn L Sullivan, Stephen Venables

Other passengers include cultural authorities Julia Child, Giancarlo Impiglia and Leroy Neiman; astronaut Buzz Aldrin, philanthropist J Paul Getty Jnr; and Titanic survivor Millvina Dean.

Hotel Manager
John Duffy

FOR QE2'S HUGELY LOYAL BAND OF TRAVELLERS ALL OVER THE WORLD, IT'S THE OVERALL EXPERIENCE OF LIFE ON BOARD AS MUCH AS THE JOURNEY THEY MAKE WHICH LIVES SO LONG IN THE MEMORY.

And for an astonishing 26 years, the overall guest experience has been the responsibility of QE2's Liverpudlian Hotel Manager John Duffy.

The former St Francis Xavier's College schoolboy, who also studied at New York's Cornell University, was appointed "Hot Man" on QE2 in 1981 – the Line's youngest ever Hotel Manager. He had earlier served on other great Cunarders including Queen Elizabeth, Carinthia, Carmania and Franconia.

At any one time onboard he can be responsible for more than 800 staff looking after as many as 1,750 guests.

It's clearly a job he relishes – and one which has rewarded him with many unforgettable memories.

"July 1990 and our first call at Liverpool has to be among the most memorable," he says.

"It was a very emotional day. I had been asking the company for many, many years before that to take the ship to Liverpool because I always felt, firstly, that it would be a very popular call which would publicise QE2 more in the area, secondly because I particularly wanted to bring her to Liverpool – I was desperate to get the ship to Liverpool, and I also felt that if QE2 went to Liverpool other ships would follow and that did actually happen."

Seventeen years after that momentous first call, other ships have indeed followed QE2's course to the Mersey. And many more will continue to do so after the Liner's 40th anniversary visit to mark the official opening of the city's cruise liner facility at Princes Parade.

"I was so pleased we had Liverpool on the 1990 itinerary and it is wonderful that so many other ships have followed," says the Hotel Manager.

"I remember coming up the river and there being so many people, it was very emotional. I was on the bridge with a reporter and they asked me why I thought there were so many spectators. That was an easy question to answer because I think virtually everybody in Liverpool has some connection with Cunard Line, whether it be an auntie, an uncle or a grandparent or a brother or sister, a cousin, whoever, somebody, sometime in the dim and distant past has worked for Cunard Line, and that's why so many people turned out to see her. Cunard Line means an awful lot to a great many people on Merseyside.

"One has to remember too, that the other Queens never came to Liverpool – the other Cunarders did of course, but not the Mary or Elizabeth, so that was the first time a Queen liner had been into the port."

Veterans of that particular voyage to celebrate Cunard Line's 150th anniversary still tell the Hotel Manager that the visit to Liverpool was the highlight of the entire trip.

"They were all bowled over by Liverpool. The American and British passengers alike. Those who have been back onboard since still talk about it as their highlight," he says.

After more than a quarter of a century's service in one of the most important positions on the most famous ship in the world, John Duffy has an unrivalled recollection of the great, the good, the rich and the famous who have visited or travelled on board.

"I've got some great, great memories of talking to various very, very well-known people," he says, discreetly declining to name names.

Places and events, as well as people, contribute to his vivid memories too.

"Another very memorable moment was when we were anchored at the Statue of Liberty for its 100th anniversary. We were the centrepiece of the most amazing and spectacular celebration. And another very memorable visit to New York was when we were the first ship back after 9/11. We sailed up the Hudson River at six o'clock on a freezing January morning, and the crowds that turned out were just incredible. There were helicopters everywhere – all around us – police and coastguard boats everywhere. It was just an amazing thing. We stopped opposite where the Twin Towers had been, and threw a wreath into the water.

HM The Queen is welcomed aboard by Hotel Manager John Duffy

Throughout, one of our entertainers sang Amazing Grace. It really was emotional. Every passenger was out on deck. We carried on slowly along the Hudson towards our pier. When we were alongside, the Mayor of New York came on board to thank us. I always recall him saying what a difference it was going to make to the city to see QE2 back. It was something I will never forget."

QE2's world cruises have become legendary. And these four-month circumnavigations of the globe have given John Duffy more memorable moments.

"Once, when we left Yokohama in Japan, there were an estimated one million spectators out to see us sail. All you could see were people, it was just incredible. Sailing into Sydney every year, even now after all these years, they turn out in their tens of thousands. As we sail in, I am just amazed that we don't knock some of the little boats under because the sea is just full of small craft. They come out in the morning and sail up into Sydney with us."

Having experienced the excitement of arriving in Sydney on board many times, John once flew out to the city to join the ship from the quayside.

"The crowds were amazing, and it was unusual for me to be on shore to experience it. The pulling power of the ship is extraordinary."

During QE2's 40th anniversary lap of honour round the United Kingdom, that pulling power will be demonstrated once again.

"It promises to be a very special and memorable event," says John Duffy. "And I am sure Liverpool will be a true highlight of the week."

Whatever the ship's reception, John Duffy will once again be striving to make sure his team provides the warmest of welcomes to everyone on board.

FINE DINING

CUNARD

40TH ANNIVERSARY 1967-2007

QE2: The Triumph of a Great Tradition

DINNER ON BOARD
QUEEN ELIZABETH 2
SATURDAY 15 SEPTEMBER 2007

THE MOST FAMOUS OCEAN LINERS IN THE WORLD™

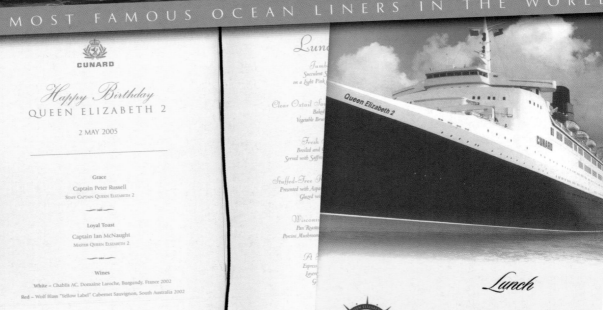

CUNARD

Happy Birthday
QUEEN ELIZABETH 2

2 MAY 2005

Grace
Captain Peter Russell
STAFF CAPTAIN QUEEN ELIZABETH 2

Loyal Toast
Captain Ian McNaught
MASTER QUEEN ELIZABETH 2

Wines

White – Chablis AC, Domaine Laroche, Burgundy, France 2002
Red – Wolf Blass "Yellow Label" Cabernet Sauvignon, South Australia 2002

Lunch

The reintroduction to service of

QUEEN ELIZABETH 2

Sunday 12 December 1999

GALA DINNER
MONDAY 26 APRIL 2004

TO CELEBRATE THE
TANDEM TRANSATLANTIC CROSSING

QUEEN MARY 2 AND QUEEN ELIZABETH 2
YORK - SOUTHAMPTON
APRIL - 1 MAY 2004

CUNARD

LUNCH ON BOARD
QUEEN ELIZABETH 2
SUNDAY 13 MAY 2007

25TH ANNIVERSARY OF THE
FALKLANDS CAMPAIGN

West Falkland
King George B.
Queen Charlotte B.
Weddell I.
Port Stephens
C. Meredith
Stanley
Choiseul Sound
Lively I.
B. of Harbours
East Falkland

HM SHIPS
ARDENT, COVENTRY AND ANTELOPE
REUNION

THE MOST FAMOUS OCEAN LINERS IN THE WORLD™

GALA DINNER   GALA DINNER
Benefitting the
Nelson Mandela
Children's Fund

Aboard
Queen Elizabeth 2
March 31st 1998

Celebration Dinner

In commemoration of the
Anniversary of the Maiden Voyage of the
RMS QUEEN MARY,
27 May 1936,
Southampton to New York

7 May 2001

CUNARD

Lunch

ON BOARD Queen Mary 2 IN SOUTHAMPTON

TO MARK THE RETIREMENT OF

COMMODORE R W WARWICK OBE, LLD, FNI

SUNDAY 30 JULY 2006

THE MOST FAMOUS OCEAN LINERS IN THE WORLD

CUNARD

Queen Elizabeth 2

...OUS OCEAN LINERS IN THE WORLD"

QUEEN ELIZABETH 2

Queen Mary

50th ANNIVERSARY

OF THE MAIDEN VOYAGE OF R.M.S. QUEEN MARY, MAY 1936.

CUNARD

*Please remember that the ship's time during the night
will be set FORWARD 60 minutes
as we pass across a world time zone.*

*Please don't forget to change your watch
before retiring ... pleasant dreams.*

Happy Birthday
QUEEN ELIZABETH 2

RECEPTION AND LUNCH ON BOARD THE
LONGEST SERVING CUNARDER EVER

TO CELEBRATE THE

36th

1969 — 2005

ANNIVERSARY OF QE2'S MAIDEN VOYAGE DEPARTURE

QUEEN ELIZABETH 2

DECK 1

8 April 2006

Queen Elizabeth 2   Queen Mary 2

MENU
RECEPTION & LUNCH
TO COMMEMORATE
THE 35TH BIRTHDAY OF
QUEEN ELIZABETH 2
AND THE TRANSFER
OF FLAGSHIP STATUS TO
RMS QUEEN MARY 2
1 MAY 2004 SOUTHAMPTON

THE MOST FAMOUS OCEAN LINERS IN THE WORLD™

WORLD CRUISES

WORLD CRUISES BECAME A HALLMARK OF QE2. Her four-month circumnavigation of the globe between January and April attracted huge interest on every sector of the voyage.

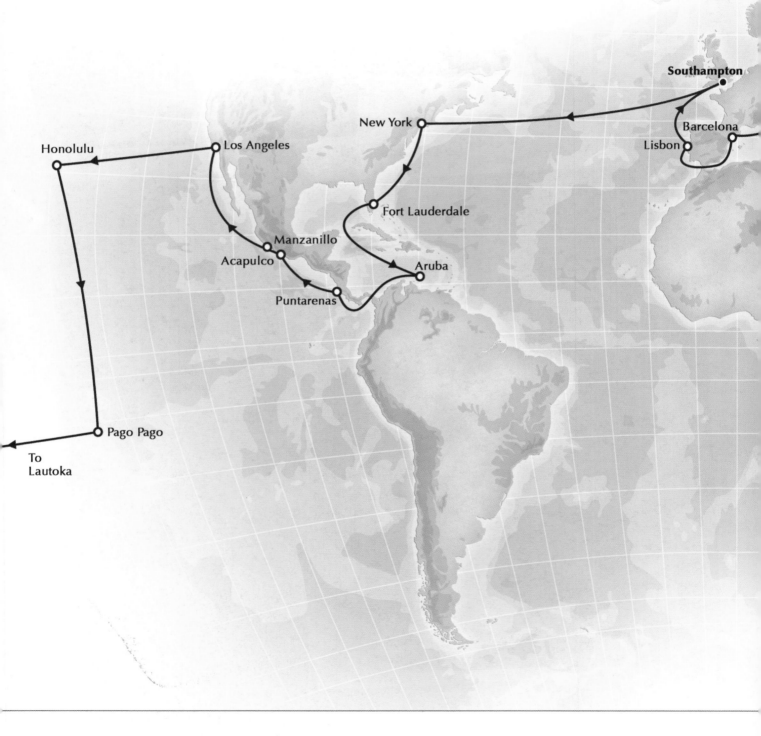

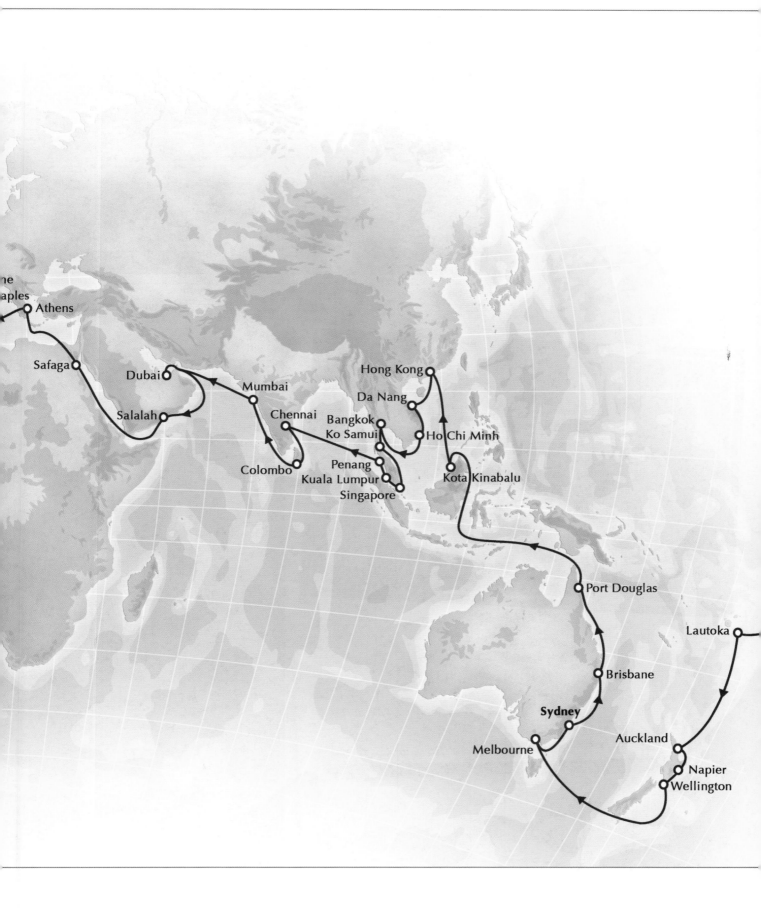

Wish
you were
here!
xxx

Geiranger, Norway

New York, New York

Greetings from
the Panama
Canal

Crosby, Merseyside

Caribbean sun

Love from Liverpool

Cape Town, SA

QE2 returns home on
June 11, 1982, after
service in the South
Atlantic

1982

FALKLANDS CAMPAIGN

A queen goes to war

WHEN HOSTILITIES BROKE OUT BETWEEN BRITAIN AND ARGENTINA over the Falkland Islands in May 1982, few envisaged a role for QE2.

They were wrong.

On May 3 as the ship passed along the south coast of England towards her home port of Southampton after another transatlantic crossing, the Government announced that it was requisitioning the British merchant flagship for war duties.

On board, there was some confusion following a BBC radio news broadcast which was made detailing the ship's role before the Captain and crew had been formally notified of her deployment.

When confirmation was flashed to the ship, Captain Alexander J. Hutcheson made a formal announcement, telling his officers and guests that the liner was being taken out of service on return to Southampton and converted for troop carrying duties.

The extensive conversion work began straight away.

Few who had travelled in cosseted comfort enjoying Cunard's legendary White Star Service could imagine the changes which the Ministry of Defence required of their favourite ship.

As the watching world was to discover during the battle in the South Atlantic, helicopters were to play a major role in the military strategy to defeat Argentine forces occupying the Islands.

QE2's open decks were cleared of their varnished steamer chairs and sun beds. Fore and aft decks were strengthened to allow helicopters to land. Major structural alterations aft included the "slicing off" of existing superstructures to create a bigger landing pad. Beneath, decks were strengthened to bear the extra weight.

As work went on round the clock on board, ashore further contingencies were being made. Most of the ship's removable décor including paintings, furniture and historic items together with crockery and glassware were packed away and stored in shore side warehouses.

Carpets facing a pounding from troops' boots were protected with hardboard and military experts installed their own top secret communications equipment in a specially adapted room behind the bridge.

After eight days and nights of frantic activity, troops finally started to embark QE2.

As she left Southampton on the afternoon of May 12, more than 3,000 members of the Fifth Infantry Brigade were settling in to their new surroundings. Sea King helicopters joined as the ship headed down the Solent and the 8,000 mile voyage to the South Atlantic was well and truly underway.

After stops at Freetown, Sierrra Leone and Ascension Island, QE2 commenced the final leg of her journey towards the war zone. News reached those on board that the Liverpool-based requisitioned container vessel Atlantic Conveyor had been lost following an air strike by Argentine forces.

By May 26, QE2 was close enough to the war zone that she started to weave rather than maintain a straight course. The ship's radar had been turned off and full blackout implemented – both orders made to lessen the risk of detection by enemy forces.

Without radar to assist navigation and with thick mist and fog forming, icebergs became a serious threat. After consultation with military commanders QE2's Captain, Peter Jackson, reactivated the ship's radar. In the hours that followed, more than 100 icebergs large enough to be picked up by radar appeared on the ship's screen.

I'm glad enemy didn't find us —captain

THE CAPTAIN of Cunard's QE2, homeward with 700 survivors of the battle for the Falklands, said yesterday his crew were "a little disappointed and surprised" to be sent back so soon.

The Argentines however had made it clear the luxury liner, which carried 3,000 troops — includ-

Troops on board QE2

After the ice threat passed, plans were made for QE2 to rendezvous with other naval vessels to commence the transfer of troops.

On the evening of May 27, QE2 dropped anchor in Cumberland Bay South Georgia about a mile from the former whaling station which weeks earlier had witnessed the start of the entire conflict.

Troops and equipment were transferred to a variety of vessels ready for the fight to regain the islands which lay 200 miles to the East.

Survivors from three sunken Royal Navy ships, HMS Ardent, HMS Antelope and HMS Coventry were taken on board QE2. Finally, on June 3, orders were received for QE2 to start her long journey home with the survivors still on board.

By June 11, QE2 was back in more familiar waters off the Isle of Wight. A tumultuous welcome home awaited with HM The Queen and HM The Queen Mother aboard the Royal Yacht Britannia to lead official recognition of Cunard Line's latest contribution to a war effort.

A message from the Queen mother was flashed to QE2.

It read: "I am pleased to welcome you back as QE2 returns to home waters after your tour of duty in the South Atlantic. The exploits of your own ship's company and the deeds of value of those who served in Antelope, Coventry and Ardent, have been acclaimed throughout the land and I am proud to add my personal tribute."

Captain Jackson replied with the words:

"Please convey to Her Majesty Queen Elizabeth our thanks for her kind message. Cunard's Queen Elizabeth 2 is proud to have been of service to Her Majesty's forces."

The two messages have been engraved in silver and can be seen on board.

QE2 was home after a mission which took her almost 15,000 miles in just under 30 days. After refitting she returned to transatlantic duty departing Southampton on August 15. Another chapter in her remarkable history was complete.

FAMOUS FEATURES

QE2'S GRACEFUL EXTERIOR LINES   helped make her one of the world's most photographed ships

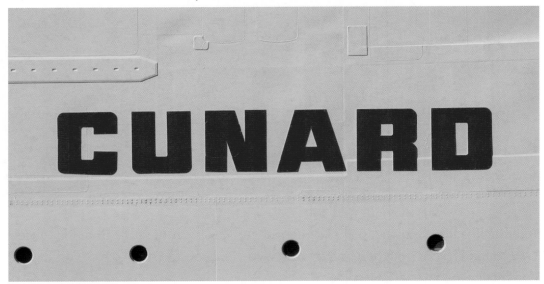

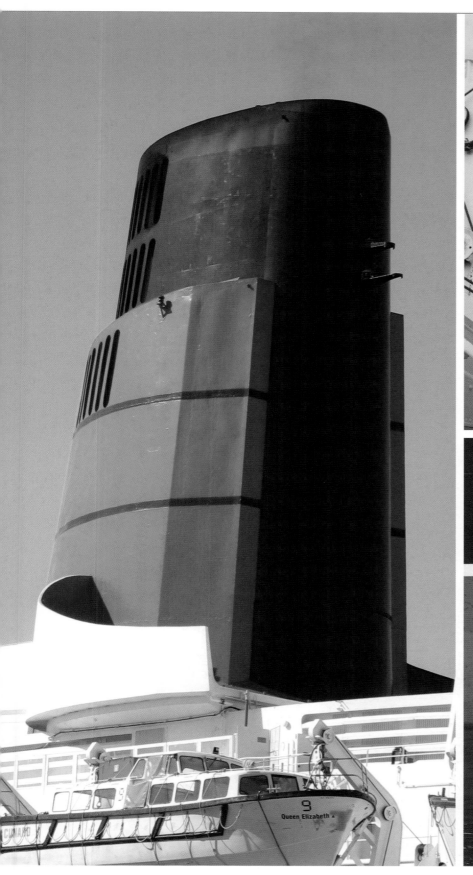

INSIDE QE2

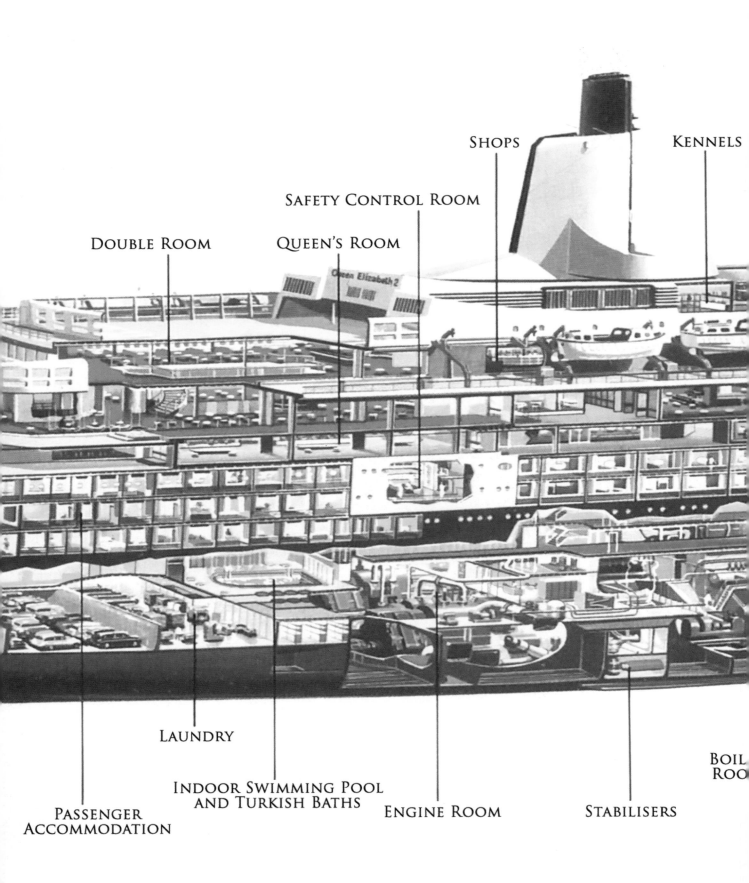

SHOPS

KENNELS

SAFETY CONTROL ROOM

DOUBLE ROOM

QUEEN'S ROOM

LAUNDRY

BOIL
ROO

INDOOR SWIMMING POOL
AND TURKISH BATHS

ENGINE ROOM

STABILISERS

PASSENGER
ACCOMMODATION

QE2

The liner as she was in the early days of her service.
Forty years at sea, and multi-million pound refits have altered her dramatically.

2 LIDO DECKS WITH OPEN-AIR SWIMMING POOLS   Q4 ROOM

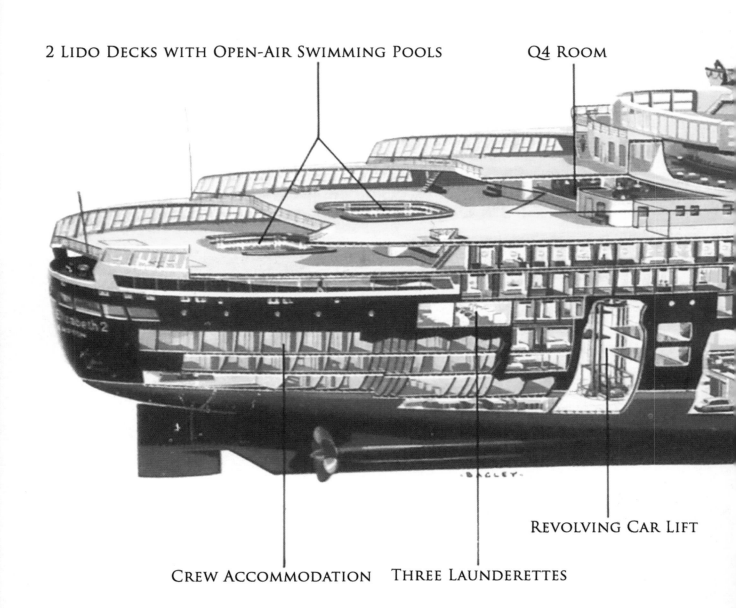

CREW ACCOMMODATION   THREE LAUNDERETTES

REVOLVING CAR LIFT

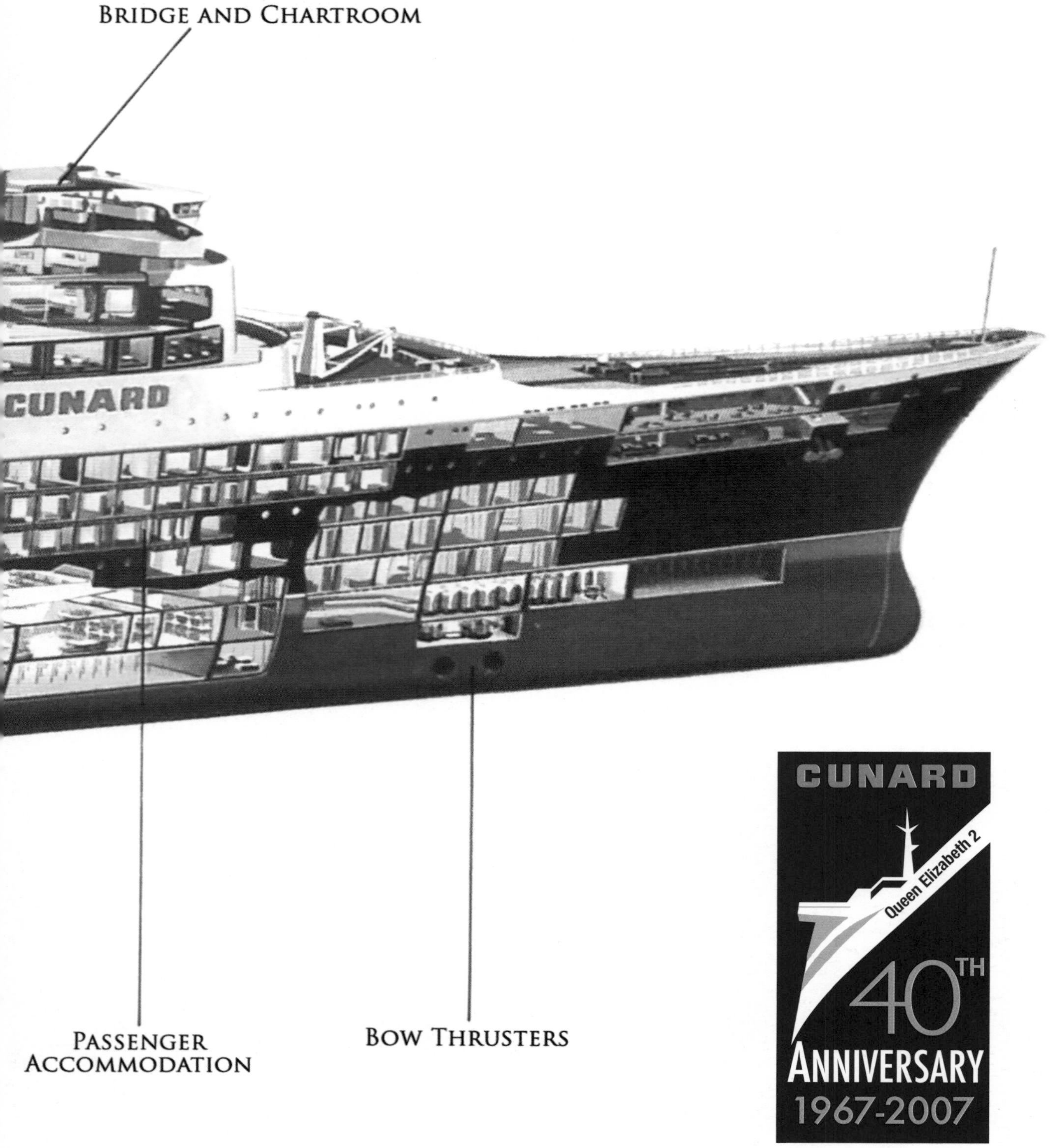

BRIDGE AND CHARTROOM

CUNARD

PASSENGER
ACCOMMODATION

BOW THRUSTERS

CUNARD

Queen Elizabeth 2

40TH

ANNIVERSARY
1967-2007

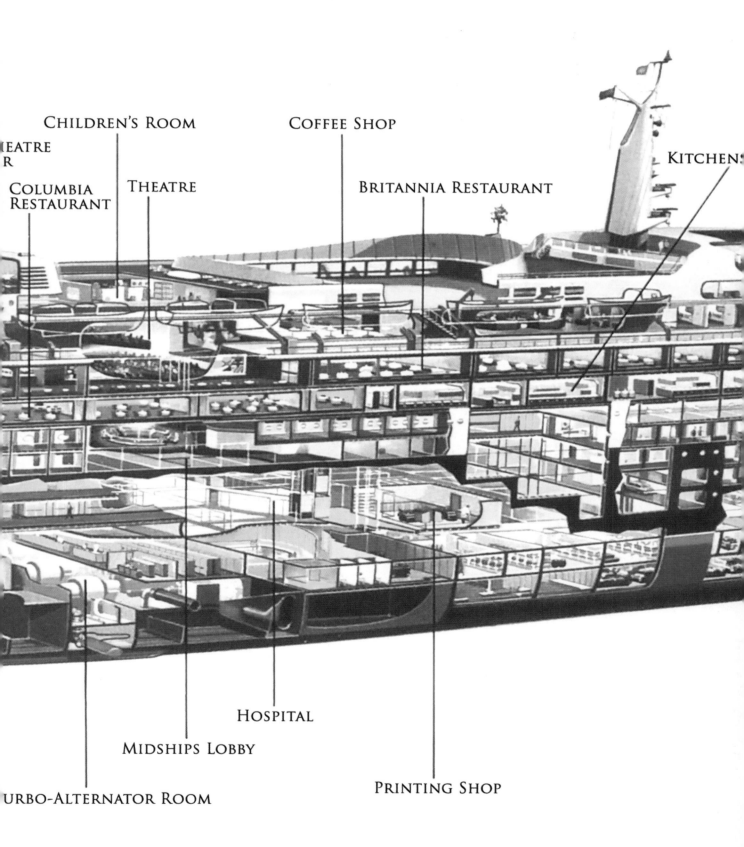

THEATRE
R

COLUMBIA
RESTAURANT

CHILDREN'S ROOM

THEATRE

COFFEE SHOP

BRITANNIA RESTAURANT

KITCHEN

HOSPITAL

MIDSHIPS LOBBY

URBO-ALTERNATOR ROOM

PRINTING SHOP

CAPTAIN ROBIN
WOODALL

THROUGHOUT HER 40 YEARS, QE2 HAS MADE HUNDREDS OF INAUGURAL CALLS AT PORTS ALL OVER THE WORLD. MANY HAVE SINCE BECOME REGULAR STOPS FOR THE LINER AS IT HAS CROSSED THE WORLD'S OCEANS.

Meticulous onboard planning and preparation must be completed before any visit to any port. When the mighty liner is calling somewhere for the first time, the arrangements need to be even more carefully thought out.

Such was the case at Liverpool in July 1990.

The responsibility for bringing what was then Cunard's flagship to the Line's spiritual home fell to Wirral resident Captain Robin Woodall.

He recalls the day clearly.

"We had the pilot on board, and I had spoken to him, obviously, about how the ship handled, and we came up to the Mersey Bar and we sat waiting there for enough water to go over the Bar, and then once there was enough water we came up the channel.

"There was quite a fresh south easterly breeze, and as we came round the Crosby turn I was looking over towards Crosby and, I remember it vividly to this day, all the sand was black. There's normally golden sand there, and I hadn't come in to the river for many a long year. I hadn't been in that position to look over at Crosby for years and years. I remarked on this to the pilot. I said it was a shame the mud has taken over from the sand. And he said, 'Oh no. That's people.'

"I looked through the binoculars, and sure enough it was people thronging the beach to watch us arrive. And that was early in the day."

The welcome continued.

"The scenes at Crosby really set the tone for the day," recalls Captain Woodall.

"New Brighton was packed solid with people, and all the way up, Seacombe, Woodside and the Pier Head were packed with crowds and crowds of spectators.

"Then of course we came to anchor and that's when the fun started because we had a screaming flood tide underneath us with the wind in the opposite direction. I had said to the pilot earlier on in the voyage when we were talking about how the ship handled, 'one thing, this ship has got four-wheel disc brakes, you know she really can stop on a dime,' and we started to swing the ship to come head to tide, and because of the tide underneath us, we were going quite quickly as we headed the bow in towards the Birkenhead dock entrance. The pilot turned to me and said: 'You said this thing had good brakes – prove it!' I did,

and we stopped, and we swung round quite happily and anchored. Then the fun continued because, wind over tide, the ship wouldn't settle. The wind was swinging her beam on to the tide, and then with the tide on the beam she was dragging because the bottom of the Mersey is not good holding ground. It's like soup. We had to keep the tugs on the ship in spite of being at anchor all morning and into the afternoon until the tide turned. The tugs just kept us stern into the wind so we didn't have the tide dragging us. When the tide turned she was perfectly alright."

The conditions prevented the Captain from leaving the bridge to attend two important ceremonies ashore – the unveiling of a bust of Sir Samuel Cunard at the Merseyside Maritime Museum and the consecration of plaques commemorating Cunard Line's war dead at Liverpool Parish Church.

"I could not go because of the way the ship was behaving, so my Staff Captain went. He got as far as the Maritime Museum, but he could not make it across to St Nicholas' because of the crowds. The place was just absolutely packed solid with people."

By late afternoon the crowds on both sides of the river were still growing.

"By the evening the breeze had dropped and we turned and swung to the flood, and the ship lay perfectly well. She was perfectly comfortable," explained the Captain.

"Come sailing time, it was really quite dramatic, the spectacle, because we heaved up the anchor, and just with a tug holding us we sat there. When the fireworks finished we set off. It was really quite dramatic –as soon as the display finished – whoosh – we'd gone. "It was a fitting demonstration of QE2's speed."

"It had been a magnificent day."

A few days earlier, under Captain Woodall's command, the liner had completed a record-breaking crossing of the North Atlantic – averaging 30.26 knots for the run from New York.

"It was quick," recalls Captain Woodall. "Four days exactly from New York to Bishop Rock lighthouse. We were fortunate with the weather conditions and I used full power the whole way across. It wasn't planned as such, it just sort of happened! We sailed from New York on schedule and my first concern was that we didn't want to be late into Southampton because that would have rebounded all the way round to the Queen coming on board. Anyway, I just don't like being late! If you say you are going to arrive somewhere, you want to get there on time. So we left New York on full power which was the nine main engines going and we were soon up to and exceeding 30 knots. We did that for two days by which time we were getting ahead of schedule, and literally I was about to go up on the bridge and tell the officer of the watch to ease back on the power, which would have meant we could have dropped an engine and saved fuel, when my phone rang and it was my contemporary in Southampton. He asked how we were doing and would we make it on time. I said I was sure we would and that we were about to start easing back. He asked if we could get in any earlier. I said yes by about five hours. So we kept full power and it was exactly four days that we went across. I've forgotten the extra price of fuel! There were no problems at all. She rattled on good style – well, she didn't rattle, she just went very quickly!"

Throughout her 40 years, QE2 has found herself in the news all over the world for all sorts of reasons.

Two of the most spectacular news events involving the ship occurred when Captain Woodall was on board.

"On one passage from New York eastbound, the Captain got a call to say there was consideration that there might be a bomb on board, because there had been this threat. Obviously, the British government and the American government took it seriously, so it was decided that they would fly out the SAS, SBS and bomb disposal, and that they duly did. They came out in a Hercules aircraft with a Nimrod above them providing all the communications links we needed. It was a horrible day, not all that rough, but with a swell of six to ten feet with very low cloud. I took the boat away from QE2. The plan was that I would get away from the ship and the Hercules would come in and drop the parachutists over me in two sticks. But then a problem occurred in that they had a minimum jump height, which was higher than the cloud. We'd dropped smoke floats so that the Hercules and the parachutists could see the wind direction. He came in over QE2, out of the cloud, saw me and the boat, and stood on his tail and climbed up back into the cloud. The first two guys jumped out and all I saw were legs appearing through the clouds. Then he came round again and the second stick came out of the aeroplane. I'd received a message as they jumped telling me that one of them was unconscious, and to make sure we picked him up first! As the pair of them appeared through the cloud we could see one of them slipping out of his 'chute first so that he could swim over to his colleague who was unconscious. They splashed in, and we belted over there to pick them up. We hauled the fellow on board and he was still unconscious. I had taken a doctor with me in the boat and he gave him a jab of some sort and the fellow came to and asked where he was. I told him he was in QE2's boat and he said: 'What? You mean I've jumped?'

Captain Woodall recalls: "He had passed out in the aeroplane because he had never jumped before! So, they pushed him out! When we got back to QE2 I escorted them to the bridge and one of them produced a newspaper from inside his wetsuit and presented it saying: 'I don't suppose you have read today's London Times?"

No explosive devices were found and QE2 arrived safely in Southampton after this drama in spring 1972.

Twenty years later the front pages of newspapers all over the world beckoned once again after QE2 struck uncharted rocks off the east coast of New England.

Captain Woodall recalls: "There was considerable damage, several gashes in the hull and lots of indentations. There was a peak of rock that was 31ft 6, I think, below the surface and we were drawing 32ft. It wasn't charted. Of course the Americans put divers down the next day and they said the rock showed signs of massive impact! Well, I bet it did after QE2 hit it at 25 knots. It split open a couple of tanks, but the bottom of the hull is quite thick!"

Thick enough and strong enough to have taken QE2 millions of miles around the world.

"Speedbird" made a
spellbinding partner for
QE2, both carrying
passengers across the
Atlantic

QE2 & CONCORDE

THROUGHOUT MUCH OF HER 40 YEARS IN SERVICE QE2 formed an unlikely alliance with another icon of British engineering and luxury travel – Concorde.

As an ocean liner conceived and created at the dawn of a jet age that, to the doubters, spelled the end of scheduled sailings of the North Atlantic, QE2 has actually outlasted the supersonic aircraft in service by more than five years.

Once the Concorde fleet was put into retirement, aircraft were shipped to various locations as permanent exhibits.

In New York, the city which hosted one of Concorde's more profitable routes, one of the aircraft sits on the deck of barge close to the USS Intrepid, a former aircraft carrier which is now a visitor attraction.

Intrepid dwarfs the Concorde and its barge and is located close to the Cunard Line's former berths on the Hudson River.

Passengers crossing from Southampton to New York in six days were often reminded of the faster way to make the journey when the British Airways "Speedbird" service from New York's JFK airport to Heathrow broke the sound barrier off the east coast of the US.

In the time it would take passengers on board the ship to conclude their daytime activities, return to their cabins and prepare for dinner following cocktails served to the accompaniment of a harpist, the Speedbird would be preparing to slow down off Britain's south west coast to commence its descent and arrival in London.

Combining the grace of a Cunard voyage with the pace of a British Airways supersonic flight held a spellbinding appeal for hundreds of travellers, and the shipping line and airline collaborated on a number of services to various ports around the world.

Closer to home, in the English Channel in 1985, QE2 participated in a photo call with a difference featuring Concorde and the RAF's aerobatic team the Red Arrows in a brilliantly co-ordinated rendezvous.

QE2 and Concorde regularly appeared together to mark special anniversaries or events – frequently involving members of the Royal Family. A Concorde fly past marked the first visit of HRH the Princess of Wales to QE2 in April 1987.

Three years later, at the climax of the QE2's round Britain voyage marking the 150th anniversary of Britannia leaving Liverpool for Canada, Concorde again made an appearance over the Solent to salute the Royal Party led by Her Majesty The Queen on board QE2.

Concorde was often chartered by Cunard to relay passengers to exotic, far flung ports of call, notably on World Cruise itineraries when guest would fly to places like Sydney or Cape Town to join their ship.

The association between the two iconic forms of transport finally ended on 24th October 2003 as Concorde flew over QE2 on the Atlantic for the last time. From the bridge, the Master of QE2 Captain Ray Heath, sent the following message to the Captain of Concorde:

"From one British icon to another: QE2 and Concorde have been an improbable, unique and successful transatlantic partnership for the past 20 years. We are sorry to see you go".

The ship herself was to carry on for another five years after Concorde's demise.

Cunard's liners maintain their traditional service to New York although Concorde (in the foreground) is now grounded

QE2 departs New York
to cross the Atlantic

ATLANTIC ADVENTURES

TO THOSE FOR WHOM GRACE rather than pace is a pre-requisite for long-haul travel, QE2 continues to offer a unique ocean-bound experience.

And nowhere has this become more evident than on the North Atlantic – a crossing from Europe to the United States of America which has been the proud domain of Cunard liners since the paddle steamer Britannia left Liverpool in 1840.

No other shipping line in the world has offered such a regular transatlantic service. And no other ship has created such lasting memories for those making this most famous and evocative journey between the continents.

The route may now belong to Queen Mary 2, but her smaller sister has created her own unique and remarkable record on the North Atlantic.

When QE2 finally ended her regular transatlantic service in May 2004 she had completed 797 crossings of the 3,500 mile route.

Her record is all the more remarkable because at the time the decision to design and build her had been taken in the Cunard Building at Pier Head, the aviation industry was promoting its jet age crossings of the Atlantic in a matter of hours rather than days.

Sceptics questioned how long Cunard could hope to sustain regular crossings between Europe and America when the airlines offered such competition. These doubts proved groundless as QE2 established herself on the route.

QE2 met Queen Mary 2 for first time in New York after completing her last westbound crossing as Cunard's flagship at the end of April 2004.

Both ships completed an historic tandem crossing back to Southampton, leaving New York in a spectacular farewell firework display off the Statue of Liberty.

2004

The ships sailed in formation down the Hudson River towards the tip of Manhattan, passing Liberty before heading under the Verrazano Narrows Bridge, and towards open water.

After passing under the bridge the ships set a course towards Nantucket Light and the vast expanse of the North Atlantic.

Six days later, the pair were in sight of Bishop Rock lighthouse off the Isles of Scilly, a point which marked the official end of the Atlantic crossing.

After passing Lands End, the ships were off Lizard Point in southern Cornwall, where the RAF saluted them during a flypast as they continued on their triumphant way to the Solent.

At a ceremony in their home port of Southampton, QM2 was officially designated Cunard Line flagship in recognition of her taking over regular transatlantic services.

The ceremony included the handing over of the Boston Cup, a magnificent silver trophy which has traditionally been carried on the Line's flagship. The Cup was received by Commodore Warwick and is now proudly displayed on board QM2.

For QE2 a major refit awaited before the next chapter in her illustrious career offered guests round trip cruise itineraries from Southampton to the Mediterranean and Northern Europe.

Queen Mary 2 (left) and QE2 leave New York together in April 2004

COMMODORE RONALD WARWICK

A HUGE PART OF QE2'S SUCCESSFUL 40 YEAR HISTORY SPANS SEPARATE PERIODS WHEN FATHER AND SON WILLIAM AND RONALD WARWICK WERE IN COMMAND OF THE VESSEL.

Birkenhead-born Commodore William E Warwick was the first Master of the ship, overseeing the final parts of construction on the Clyde before taking delivery from John Brown's shipyard – and overall command of the liner.

His son Captain Ronald Warwick followed him to the post in 1990. Some 13 years later, in command of the world's largest liner Queen Mary 2, Captain Warwick was himself promoted to the position of Commodore of Cunard Line – marking a unique family achievement.

Childhood memories of Liverpool and the Mersey remain clear for Commodore Ronald Warwick.

"My earliest recollections are when I was about seven years old, and we used to be taken on the overhead railway by my grandmother who was the manager of the Lord Nelson Hotel near Lime Street Station," explains the recently retired Commodore.

"I did not become aware of QE2 until my father was appointed as the Master Designate in the mid-1960s. At the time I was a Second Mate on a cargo ship, the Jamaica Producer, and the radio Officer told me he had read about the appointment when he received the daily news by Morse code. On my return to London, I collected all the press cuttings about my father, and subsequently became interested in the ship itself. Ever since, and up to the present day, I have kept and filed press cuttings and articles about QE2.

Included in this unique collection are reports of the liner's first call at Liverpool in July 1990.

"I was on board as a supernumerary Master understudying Captain Robin Woodall. I remember being in awe of the welcome we received from the public, and how exciting it was sailing up the Mersey and seeing all the magnificent buildings steeped in heritage. In particular, looking at the Cunard Building, I found myself thinking of the paddle steamer Britannia sailing from Liverpool on her maiden voyage across the North Atlantic on the 4th July 1840," says Commodore Warwick.

After the historic first call, QE2 has returned to the Mersey on a number of occasions.

One, above all others, remains firm in Commodore Warwick's mind.

"My second visit to the port was in 1995 by which time I was in command. On this occasion, my father was on board as a passenger. Having been brought up in Liverpool, this was a very special visit for him. He shared many of his reminiscences with me as we stood together on the bridge. He could just see the place he was born – the Royal Hotel on the banks of the Mersey near Rock Ferry. As with the first visit in 1990, another of the most vivid memories is of the welcome we received from the people of the city and elsewhere.

The welcome and the send off were equally spectacular with thousands of people on both sides of the Mersey seeing us on our way."

After a lifetime sailing into ports all over the world, Commodore Warwick says Liverpool has a host of attractive features.

"One of the most attractive features about Liverpool as a port is that fact that we anchor, and soon berth alongside, in the heart of the city. In many ports around the world, QE2 has to berth in the industrial areas of the harbour. To be near the architectural heart of the city on the World Heritage Site waterfront is a fitting place for the Queen to be," he says.

Like others in command of QE2 during visits to the Mersey, Commodore Warwick recalls busy days spent sat mid river with Mersey Ferries tendering guests to and from the shore.

"Any port where we have to use tenders requires extra care and diligence from our crew. However, Liverpool was often more demanding because of the strong tidal stream, and the fact that the holding ground of the river bed is not ideal for such a large liner, and dragging of the anchor is likely to occur, especially when the tide turns."

Liverpool may be considered the birthplace of Cunard Line's scheduled transatlantic services, and QE2's visits to the Mersey have always served to reinforce the bond between the Line and the city.

"Seeing QE2 in the Mersey, in front of the Cunard Building is a remarkable site. The ship really has become an icon. QE2 was unique when she came into service, and I think that this uniqueness, coupled with the fact that, within a few years of her maiden voyage, she was the only ship making regular Atlantic crossings, has made her an icon."

As well as being able to sail with his father, the ship's first Master, there are many other memorable moments in the Warwick family history linked to QE2.

"I performed the wedding ceremony of my daughter Rebecca when we were docked in Boston, USA. That was believed to be the first legal marriage carried out by the Master on a British registered ship," recalls the Commodore.

In all his years on board QE2 and other Cunard vessels, Commodore Warwick has met many of the Line's most loyal and appreciative passengers and guests, many of whom have returned to the ship time after time.

"The Cunard mission has always been to encourage repeat passengers by providing excellent and memorable service. Considerable resources are devoted to crew training, especially in encouraging the crew to develop team work among themselves to ensure they deliver the best possible service to each other and their passengers."

The Commodore believes this approach helps attract Cunard guests back on board.

When Commodore Warwick left QE2 to take command of Queen Mary 2 before its launch and Maiden Voyage, there were inevitably those who felt the older liner's days were numbered.

Now QE2's retirement plans are known, the Commodore is sure Queen Mary 2 will become as successful an icon as her older sister.

"QE2 was unique when she came into service. Now QM2 is well on the way to becoming an icon too. When QE2 retires, QM2's status will just go from strength to strength on the Atlantic Ocean."

The Commodore supports the way QE2's new owners are planning to take her into retirement.

"However, my own personal wish for the destiny of the ship was for it to remain with Cunard Line's parent company the Carnival Corporation. I envisaged the Corporation setting up a separate entity to operate the ship in a permanent berth in Florida in a similar way to the Queen Mary in California. It could have been a museum for the shipping lines owned by the Corporation, and a library and learning centre for everything associated with the cruise industry."

"From what I have seen and heard, it sounds as though the new owners are very motivated to preserve the ship in the way many wish her to be remembered."

The Commodore will not be alone in hoping that is the case.

July 24 1990: QE2's first
call at Liverpool drew
thousands to the waterside

FIRST VISIT TO LIVERPOOL

TUESDAY, JULY 24TH, 1990 was a momentous day for Cunard Line and Liverpool.

Exactly 150 years after Sir Samuel Cunard's transatlantic service was launched when the paddle steamer Britannia left the Mersey bound for Halifax, Nova Scotia and Boston, the Line's flagship QE2 was making her maiden call.

Just as the departure of Britannia had captured the imagination of the city on July 4th 1840, so the arrival of the most famous ship in the world triggered a day and night of celebration on both banks of the river – and, for those lucky enough to experience them, a series of lavish celebratory events on board.

By the time QE2 sailed late that evening, official estimates calculated that more than 1million people had turned out to see her arrive and drop anchor in the middle of the Mersey.

The perfect summer's day has since gone down in local history as one of the city's most memorable.

It started early for a group of VIPs who flew by helicopter to meet the ship close to the Mersey Bar.

After their short flight passengers caught their first glimpse of the mighty liner heading for Liverpool.

The helicopter touched down on board and excited guests disembarked their aircraft to begin their momentous voyage up the Mersey.

Civic leaders and other guests received a formal welcome on board.

QE2 weighed anchor just before midnight amid a huge firework display

1990

The previous day, during this special passage commemorating the Line's 150th anniversary, QE2 had called at Cobh in Ireland.

Calls at Greenock and Cherbourg were to follow the Liverpool stop as the commemorative tour of the UK and Ireland headed back to Southampton.

On the bridge, officers reached for their binoculars to view Crosby beach and soon realised this was to be a very special day.

Thousands of well-wishers were already lining the shore to greet the ship.

Similar scenes were visible across the river towards Fort Perch Rock at New Brighton and all the way along the promenade to Seacombe.

As the crowds gathered ashore, the river became busy too as a flotilla of small craft turned out to add their welcome.

QE2 was to drop anchor mid river, opposite the Cunard Building where a tender service was to be operated by Mersey Ferries bringing passengers ashore at the Pier Head.

Tugs deployed to assist played a spectacular part in the welcome by firing their water jets in salute to the liner as she edged closer to her mooring for the day.

As more helicopters and other light aircraft buzzed above, the scene was set for a memorable day of celebration.

By lunchtime, the numbers lining the river at Pier Head were swelled by hundreds of office workers drawn to the water's edge to catch a glimpse of the ship.

Impromptu picnics and parties started on both sides of the river as families enjoyed the sunshine and the spectacle.

The Mersey Ferries were packed for each of their special cruises throughout the day and tickets for an evening excursion to coincide with QE2's departure had sold out weeks before.

At lunchtime, ferry passengers witnessed the spectacular release of 10,000 balloons from the ship's Quarter Deck to mark the inaugural call at Liverpool.

As the day unfolded, more and more people made their way to the waterside and by the time the ship was ready to depart at around 11pm the stage was set for a spectacular firework display.

With a medley of Beatles songs and a rousing replay of Gerry Marsden's famous anthem Ferry 'Cross the Mersey, QE2 weighed anchor and edged slowly away from her position in front of the Pier Head.

Thousands of flashguns popped as the final fireworks lit the sky and the ship saluted the city with several blasts on her whistle.

Some 23 years had passed since Cunard Line closed its former Liverpool headquarters, and it had taken the same time for the Line's flagship to make her maiden call at her spiritual home.

Those who witnessed the day's events will always be a part of Merseyside's maritime history.

CAPTAIN IAN
McNAUGHT

QE2'S HISTORIC 40TH ANNIVERSARY CALL AT
LIVERPOOL WILL MARK A NOSTALGIC RETURN TO
THE PORT FOR HER MASTER.

Captain Ian McNaught started his sea-going career with BP
before joining another of Liverpool's world famous shipping
companies, Bibby Line, in 1976.

Captain McNaught had spent four years serving on board BP
tankers before his move to Bibby Line saw him join vessels
trading between the Gulf, Singapore and Hong Kong.

In 1976, having had enough of oil tankers and petroleum gas
ships working deep sea, Captain McNaught joined a British
company running a small fleet of coastal tankers.

He made his move into passenger shipping by joining Cunard
in 1987, on QE2 as Second Officer.

After two years he was transferred to Cunard Princess as First
Officer and spent several months in Bahrain when the ship
served as a rest base for American service personnel in the first
Gulf War.

He rejoined QE2 in 1991 and was subsequently promoted to
Chief Officer, then Staff Captain before, in 2003, at the age of
48, becoming QE2's youngest Master.

His memories of the ship go back his schoolboy days in
Sunderland.

"My first memory, as a little boy, was writing to people at Cunard and John Brown and asking for any information and putting it all in a scrap book. I was about nine or 10 when it was announced that Cunard was ordering a new liner and I was fascinated," recalls the Captain.

"I lost the scrap book – and now that would have been a real treasure. There was all sorts in it. I wrote to everybody and filled it with the things I got back. Then one day it just disappeared; I don't know what I did with it."

Despite being the youngest Master appointed to command QE2 – and losing his scrapbook – Captain McNaught can remember television coverage of the ship being launched.

"I was 12 at the time, so now to be here, is a little boy's dream come true. It's great when you board QE2 because you meet people who, in some tiny way, were involved in the building of her. There were two ladies on board recently who worked in the drawing office at the shipyard, and we still have a lot of the original drawings on board. When they came up here for the cocktail party I said to them they must have seen some changes on board. They said they had never been on board before. Women were not allowed on the ship in the yard because it was still considered unlucky. Forty years later, here they are, doing a cruise, enjoying every minute."

In the months leading up to QE2's 40th Anniversary, the Captain has met many passengers longing for the chance to sail on the special celebratory cruise round the UK. "The interest has been amazing. I have spoken to lots of passengers who have said they wished they had known about the itinerary. I think there is something special for a lot of British passengers to be able to sail around the entire coastline of their own country – and when the journey is on board QE2 at such a special time, it's bound to be even more memorable."

He adds: "It's going to be a fantastic week. It's going to be a busy week too. The crew are really looking forward to it. For the passengers, I think it's just going to be one big old party! And the places we go to will, I am sure, take on board just how special

the week is – which is wonderful because it's never going to happen again for her 40th Anniversary. With the greatest respect to Queen Mary 2, I don't think there will ever be another atmosphere like we have on here really."

And what does QE2's current Master think makes his ship so special?

"What we have got here is a proper Atlantic liner. People come here because when they step inside they know they are in a ship, they get a real shipboard experience, and I think the relationship people have with the crew is so special. It's all down to people in the end, it's all down to the boys and girls downstairs who work so hard to make it what it is. It's a ship with a heart and a soul."

Captain McNaught is relishing the prospect of being able to bring the ship alongside Liverpool's new liner berth during the historic call at Cunard's former home.

"It'll be wonderful to be alongside during a Liverpool call. Mooring mid-river is a challenge because such a strong tide runs up and down the Mersey. It's really difficult, and you watch those Ferries and they are going sideways, backwards and forwards. Last time we went, there was a big, big tide running and to get this turned round in a flood tide so she could stem the tide was phenomenal. There were four tugs working with us that day, but that's the way that river is. But this time, to be able to go alongside the Landing Stage like lots of our predecessors did will be wonderful. It's a huge step forward, and of course that's got to be great for the City of Liverpool because it now becomes a much more attractive proposition for other cruise ships to call there."

QE2's ninth and final visit to Liverpool will take place on Friday, October 3rd 2008.

It promises to be another memorable day.

QE2 FACTS AND FIGURES

Often dubbed a floating hotel, QE2 is in fact far more like a complete city at sea.

QE2 is eight times longer than the Statue of Liberty is high (111 feet), three times as long as Big Ben (310 feet), as long as 30 double-decker London buses (31½ feet each), more than twice as long as St Paul's Cathedral (366 feet), and only 21 feet shorter than the height of the Eiffel Tower (984 feet).

Other facts and figures from this floating city include:

PASSENGER CAPACITY: 1787

DECKS: 13

PASSENGER DECKS: 12

LIFTS: 13 Passenger, 2 (former) Car, 8 Store, 1 Engine Room

CONSUMPTION AND STORES

	DAILY	ANNUALLY
Tea Bags	2,500 bags	912,500 bags
Coffee	100 lbs	16.5 tons
Cooking oil	50 gallons	18,250 gallons
Eggs	3,200	1,168,000
Milk	230 gallons	83,950 gallons
Butter	350 lbs	58 tons
Breakfast cereal	770 packets	281,050 packets
Marmalade / jam	553 portions	201,050 portions
Bananas	230 lbs	38 tons
Strawberries	125 lbs	20 tons
Fruit juice	640 gallons	233,600 gallons
Tomatoes	120lbs	43,800 lbs
Smoked salmon	30 kilos	11 tons
Caviar	6.6 lbs	2,409 lbs
Lobster	116 lbs	42,340 lbs
Strip loin	450 lbs	164,250 lbs
Flour	753 lbs	122 tons
Rice	380 lbs	62 tons
Potatoes	694 lbs	62 tons
Saffron	1.5 packets	547.5 packets
Beer	2,400 bottles	5,309 gallons
Spirits	180 litres	65,700 litres
Champagne	200 bottles	73,000 bottles
Wine	370 bottles	135,050 bottles
Soft drinks	820 bottles	299,300 bottles
Cigarettes	1000 packets	365,000 packets
Cigars	41 boxes	12,425 boxes
Doilies		Over 2 million
Napkins and Cocktail Stirrers		Over 1 million each
Alumium Foil		125 miles

- QE2 sends all its used cooking oil ashore for reconstituting into animal feed.
- 277,000 metres of cling film is used very year, enough to go around the Queen Elizabeth 2 nearly 731 times.
- Heineken and Becks together account for almost 50% of the beer consumed.
- Pound for pound, the most expensive food item on board is saffron (2.5 times the value of Beluga caviar).
- The number of tea bags used each day would supply a family for an entire year.
- To eat QE2's daily consumption of breakfast cereal, two people would have to eat at least one packet a day for more than a year.
- Enough fruit juice is used in one year to fill up QE2's swimming pools nearly 8 times.
- Approximately 600,000 litres of beverage are consumed annually.
- If all the cigarettes smoked annually on board (6.5 million) were placed in a line, the line would be 370 miles long which is equivalent to the distance from London to Edinburgh.
- On a six-day transatlantic crossing, the following beverages are consumed: Gin - 600 bottles (7 brands), Rum - 240 bottles (5 brands), Vodka - 129 bottles (3 brands), Brandy - 240 bottles (10 brands), Liqueurs - 360 bottles (18 types), Sherry - 240 bottles (5 brands), Port - 120 bottles (4 brands), Fruit Juice - 25,720 cans

ACCOMMODATION

PASSENGER STATEROOMS:

Total number of staterooms:	947
Outside doubles	636
Outside singles	32
Inside doubles	204
Inside singles	75
Staterooms-equipped for disabled passengers	4

QUEEN MARY AND QUEEN ELIZABETH GRAND SUITES

QE2's two ultra-luxurious 'Grand Suites', named after the most illustrious Cunarders, are among the largest and most lavish suites afloat. Each 1,184-square foot Grand Suite was decorated in creams, beiges, light woods and feature a bedroom with private veranda, complete with walk-in closet and marble bathroom. A double door leads to a dining area, which in turn adjoins a raised lounge, leading to a glass-covered conservatory and private, forward-facing deck area.

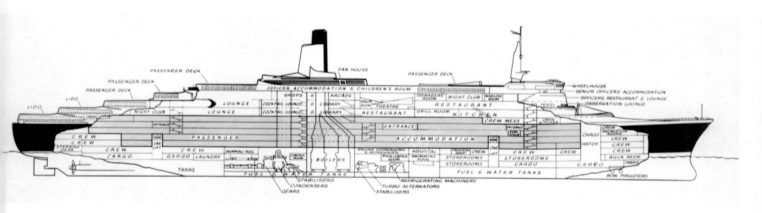

THE SHIP'S COMPANY:

Crew	approximately 1016
Nationality of Officers	Mainly British
Nationality of Staff	International

Captain	1	Fitness Instructors	1
Staff Captain	1	Florists	1
Hotel Manager	1	Gentlemen Hosts	10
Chief Engineer	1	Hairdressers	13
Purser	1	Hotel Officers	35
Cruise Director	1	Kitchen Supervisors	2
Administration Assistant	1	Laundry Staff	17
Assistant Restaurant Managers	12	Librarians	2
Baggage Masters	2	Linenkeeper	1
Bank Staff	3	Lido Supervisor	4
Barkeepers	17	Masters at Arms	4
Beauticians	2	Medical Dispenser	1
Bedroom Stewards/esses	69	Night Stewards	6
Bell Boy	2	Nursery Nurses	2
Bosun	1	Nursing Sisters	3
Bosun's Mate	1	Orchestra Staff	23
Casino Staff	16	Personnel Manager	1
Chefs De Cuisine	5	Photographers	4
Chefs/Sous-Chefs	107	Printers	4
Commis Waiters	13	Public Room Steward/esses	25
Crew Administration Assistant	1	Public Room Supervisor	1
Crew Cooks	2	Radio Officers	1
Cruise Sales Manager	2	Radio Officer Assistants	3
Cruise Staff	9	Security Officer	1
Dancers	10	Secretaries	3
Data Input Clerks	5	Shop Assistants	18
Deck Officers	10	Staff Bedroom Steward	6
Deck Ratings	36	Store Managers	3
Deck Supervisors	9	Storekeepers	5
DJ	1	Tour Staff	3
Doctors	2	TV Manager	1
Engineering Officers	26	Utility Staff	182
Engine Ratings	65	Waiters/Waitresses	1175
Entertainers	5	Assistant Waiters	9
Executive Chef	1	Wine Stewards/esses	22

GENERAL INFORMATION

KEEL LAID:	4 July 1965
LAUNCHED:	20 September 1967
	by Her Majesty Queen Elizabeth II
BUILT BY:	John Brown and Co. (Clydebank) Ltd, Scotland; later Upper Clyde Shipbuilders
COST:	£8,825,185
MAIDEN VOYAGE:	2 May 1969
	Southampton to New York
PORT OF REGISTRY:	Southampton, England.
SIGNAL LETTERS:	G.B.T.T.
OFFICIAL NUMBER:	336703

VITAL STATISTICS

TONNAGES

Gross:	70,327
Net:	37,182
Deadweight:	11,590

LENGTHS

Overall:	963 feet (293.53 metres)
Bridge to Stem:	282 feet 2.5 inches (86 metres)
Bridge to Stern:	724 feet10 inches (220 metres)
BREADTH:	105 feet 2.5 inches (32.06 metres)
DRAUGHT:	32 feet 7.5 inches (9.94 metres)

HEIGHTS

Mast head above Keel:	200 feet 1.5 inches (61 metres)
Funnel above Keel:	204 feet 1.5 inches (62.2 metres)
Masthead above Sea Level:	167 feet 1 inch (51.054 metres)
Funnel:	69 feet 6 inches (21.2 metres)
Bridge Height of Eye:	95 feet (29 metres)

SPEED

Maximum	32.5 knots
Service	25 - 28.5 knots

FUEL CONSUMPTION

18.05 tonnes per hour, or 433 tonnes per day.

❖ This is equal to six of the ship's swimming pools.

❖ The ship's fuel oil tank capacity of 4,381.4 tonnes is sufficient for 10 days' sailing at 32.5 knots, equalling 7,800 miles.

❖ One gallon of fuel will move the ship 49.5 feet; with the previous steam turbine engines, one gallon of fuel moved the ship 36 feet.

TANK CAPACITIES

Fresh Water	1,852.0 tonnes
Laundry Water	489.0 tonnes
Diesel Oil	206.8 tonnes
Fuel Oil	4,381.4 tonnes
Lubricating Oil	335.7 tonnes
Ballast	4,533.0 tonnes
Feed Water	113.8 tonnes

WATER PRODUCTION / CONSUMPTION

❖ Four Serck vacuum flash evaporators, producing 250 tonnes each per day.

❖ One reverse osmosis plant producing 450 tonnes.

❖ Total production - 1,450 tonnes per day.

❖ Consumption - about 1,000 tonnes per day; equivalent to 14 of the ship's swimming pools.

STOPPING CAPABILITY

❖ The ship can reduce speed from 32.5 knots full ahead to standstill in 3 minutes 39 seconds, in a distance of 0.75 nautical miles (1.39 km).

❖ The ship can go from standstill to full speed astern (19 knots) in 12 minutes.

EXTERIOR

THE FUNNEL

This is the most recognisable feature of QE2, the funnel is 69 feet high and is one of the most efficient and practical designs in any passenger liner.

THE MAST

The mast structure performs the useful functions of clearing waste gases from the main kitchen, and carries the radar scanners, aerials and navigation lights.

AND FINALLY...QE2 HAS:

❖ 2,252 light fixtures in passenger areas

❖ 74,200 square yards of chair and curtain fabric

❖ 1,350 portholes

❖ 577 windows

❖ The most powerful propulsion plant on a non-military vessel

❖ The most extensive medical facilities after a hospital ship

QE2 LUXURY

THROUGHOUT HER 40 YEARS, official classifications have consistently rated service, accommodation and facilities on board QE2 as among the finest in the world.

Her maiden calls at ports all over the world have generated huge local interest. Her arrivals and departures regularly attract thousands of people to shore side vantage points even in those ports where she has become a regular and familiar sight.

For many of those lining the world's port approaches and breakwaters QE2 epitomises a type of travel from a bygone age.

Many aspire to one day travel on board and savour the experience for themselves.

By November 2004, QE2 had welcomed almost 3 million passengers on board having completed 35 years, six months and three days in service and reached a memorable milestone in her life by becoming the longest serving Cunard express liner in the company's history.

QE2 took the record from the Aquitania which served Cunard Line, in peace and war, from May 1914 to December 1949.

So what have almost 3 million passengers come to expect and enjoy once on board QE2?

Passengers preparing to embark in her home port of Southampton immediately appreciate the special atmosphere as they enter the Queen Elizabeth II terminal.

Some may have arrived by rail on board the special Cunard chartered Orient Express service from London, their train drawing to a halt immediately outside the terminal.

Others step from chauffer driven limousines, taxis or coaches. Porters bustle about well aware that their task is time critical if the liner hidden from view by the departure terminal is to sail on time.

Inside the large reception area Cunard shore staff and ship's crew are on hand to offer immediate assistance. Orderly queues of passengers are checked in quickly and invited to ascend to the main departure lounge above the check in hall.

All the time, the behind the scenes preparations for their voyage – both on board and ashore elsewhere in the terminal – are continuing.

After a short while embarkation begins and guests are invited to pass through their final security checks before boarding the ship.

At the gangway, official photographers are on hand to record the moment guests start to live their long-held dreams by boarding the most famous ship in the world.

As a band plays on the quayside, guests step from the gangway into QE2's magnificent Midships Lobby where a harpist plays and an impeccably dressed line of white-gloved stewards and stewardesses is on hand to escort guests to their staterooms.

Such is the warmth of this welcome (and the enthusiasm of the crew members to see their guests to their accommodation), the style, elegance and Cunard Line history exhibited in the furnishings and displays of Midships Lobby can be momentarily missed by wide-eyed passengers as they are whisked on their way.

The main accommodation is housed on decks 5,4,3,2 and 1 in a variety of well-appointed cabins and staterooms.

Unlike modern cruise ships, QE2 has a small ratio of suites with balconies – she was after all designed for crossing the North Atlantic in storm force conditions when private balcony areas would be of little use and could even be dangerous.

2004

On board today, QE2 has two ultra luxurious Grand Suites, named after illustrious sister ships Queen Mary and Queen Elizabeth, and are among the most lavish suites afloat.

Each 1,184-square foot Grand Suite is decorated in creams, beiges and light woods and feature a bedroom with private veranda, complete with walk-in closet and marble bathroom. A double door leads to a dining area, which in turn adjoins a raised lounge, leading to a glass-covered conservatory and private, forward-facing deck area. A butler is on hand to attend to guests individual requirements.

In these lavish surroundings guests can enjoy eating and entertaining in their own private dining room, or in the Queens Grill Restaurant – widely acknowledged to be one of the finest dining experiences available in the world – on land or at sea.

QE2 has two other fine dining facilities in the Princess and Britannia Grills as well as two larger restaurants – the Caronia and the Mauritania. In addition The Lido Restaurant offers an informal buffet and self service catering; The Golden Lion

(named after Cunard's lion rampant emblem) provides traditional pub grub and a room service menu is available 24 hours a day.

Ascending from the main accommodation decks, QE2 expansive public rooms are laid out on the Quarter, Upper and Boat Decks.

Step from the lift on Quarter Deck for the elegant surroundings of the 554-seater Caronia Restaurant. The last Cunard Line ship to bear this evocative title was named at a ceremony in Liverpool in December 1998. Today, this restaurant is one of the most popular on board QE2.

Elsewhere on Quarter Deck is QE2's famous Library and Bookshop. The Library shelves stock 6,000 books and two full-time Librarians are on board to assist guests making their selections.

The ship's main ballroom, The Queens Room, is also located on Quarter Deck. Its striking focal point is a bust of Her Majesty Queen Elizabeth II.

As well as hosting dancing and concerts, the Queens Room is one of the most popular venues for another fine Cunard tradition – Afternoon Tea served at 4pm prompt.

Behind The Queens Room is The Chart Room bar where valuable navigational artefacts from other Cunarders are displayed together with a finely crafted chest of drawers containing sets of Admiralty Charts. Guest entertainers play the magnificent maple piano which was once located on board Queen Mary.

The Chart Room's focal point is a large etched glass panel behind the bar which shows two navigation courses across the North Atlantic.

Elsewhere on Quarter Deck is the entrance to The Lido Restaurant; a Cruise Sales Office where guests can plan and book future itineraries and Club 2000, part of on board facilities for children and teenage passengers.

Rising through the decks, next is Upper Deck where some of QE2's grandest facilities and public rooms can be found including the 530-seat Mauretania Restaurant and popular Crystal Bar. Stairs from Upper Deck also give access to the smaller and more exclusive Britannia and Princess Grill Restaurants. Each has a capacity to accommodate around 100 guests in sumptuous and elegant surroundings.

Along the wide, window lined thoroughfares of Upper Deck lie the Golden Lion pub, The Casino, the 529-seater Theatre/Cinema, a Photo Shop and Gallery and The Grand Lounge – the ship's main stage entertainment area which can accommodate 590 passengers. Upper Deck aft lies the Yacht Club bar and lounge with direct access to open decks.

One deck above on Boat Deck, QE2's expansive open decks can be accessed. Five laps of the deck is a distance of one mile. For those less intent on daily exercise, teak recliners along the ship's rails provide restful and relaxing vantage points to watch the oceans pass by.

The outdoor Sports Court with tennis, basketball, golf and shuffleboard facilities is also on Boat Deck.

Indoors is the Royal Promenade shopping mall which includes a branch of Harrods, the Theatre/Cinema Circle or Gallery and QE2's finest restaurant, the 231-seater Queens Grill and Queens Grill Lounge and Bar reserved for the exclusive use of Grill passengers.

The QE2's Boardroom is also located on Boat Deck and can be used for private receptions, card schools or meetings.

Outside on Boat Deck, stairs lead guests to the former helicopter landing site on Sun Deck. Safety regulations prevent helicopters landing on the deck now, and a new café and Funnel Bar area has been created.

Other luxurious facilities on board QE2 include a hair and beauty salon on 1 Deck; indoor and outdoor pools, a gymnasium, a thalassotherapy pool, sauna and steam room. Guests can also visit the computer centre for email and Internet access, a laundrette, florist and the Travellers' Cove store and gift shop.

In all, a real city at sea!

QE2 SISTER SHIPS

CUNARD LINE WAS FORMED IN 1839 PRINCIPALLY TO CARRY THE ROYAL MAIL BETWEEN THE UK AND NORTH AMERICA, AND IN DOING SO INAUGURATED IN 1840 THE FIRST TIMETABLED STEAMSHIP SERVICE ACROSS THE ATLANTIC. THE COMPANY NOW OPERATES THE LAST SCHEDULED SERVICE.

Cunard's current fleet consists of RMS Queen Mary 2 and Queen Elizabeth 2. The 90,000-ton Queen Victoria will join the fleet in December 2007.

QUEEN MARY 2 entered service on 12 January 2004 and made worldwide headlines. Queen Mary 2 is the first transatlantic liner to be built since QE2 and is the only liner offering a scheduled transatlantic service.

Queen Mary 2 is:

* the biggest (151,400-tons)

* the longest (1,132 feet / 342 metres),

* the tallest (236 feet / 72 metres),

* the widest (135 feet / 41 metres) passenger liner ever and, at a cost of £540 million, was, on entering service, the most expensive passenger ship in history.

Queen Mary 2 quickly established herself as a destination in her own right. Everything about this ship is superlative and she offers a whole host of 'firsts' and exclusives.

* 79% of staterooms feature private balconies.

* There is over £3.5 million of artwork on board.

* The world's first floating Planetarium offers virtual reality rides through the galaxy.

QUEEN MARY 2 AND QE2 WILL BE JOINED IN DECEMBER 2007 BY CUNARD'S NEWEST LINER, QUEEN VICTORIA.

The liner design of Queen Victoria has provided the ship's interior designers with more space in terms of height and volume. Queen Victoria's Cunard heritage will be reflected in the design of the grand, elegant and intimate public areas.

❖ First impressions matter and Queen Victoria will impress as soon as guests embark into the ship's three-storey Grand Lobby which will be decorated in mahogany and marble.

❖ Queen Victoria's two-deck Queen's Room is the ballroom and is designed for dancing, cocktail parties and traditional English afternoon tea.

The room will feature a dramatic high ceiling, crystal chandeliers, a large dance floor with inlaid wood patterns and backlit glass panels.

❖ With its retractable glass roof, The Winter Garden will be Queen Victoria's indoor / outdoor relaxation area and will be reminiscent of a grand conservatory complete with fountain.

❖ Queen Victoria will offer a whole range of bars and clubs (13 in total) to suit a wide variety of tastes and provide a range of atmospheres, including a traditional English Pub (the Golden Lion), a Champagne Bar, a nautically-themed cocktail bar (The Chart Room) and the relaxing Midships Lounge.

❖ With its 270-degree views, Queen Victoria's Hemispheres will be situated on top of the ship (10 Deck) overlooking the Pavilion Pool.

❖ The 6,000 book traditionally-styled English Library, situated on 2 and 3 Decks, will be a double-deck room with rich mahogany wood paneling, stained glass, leather sofas and armchairs and a spiral staircase. The area will have two full-time Librarians in attendance.

❖ Queen Victoria will even feature a floating museum called Cunardia that will display a unique collection of Cunard memorabilia and artifacts.

FAREWELL QUEEN OF THE SEAS

THE END OF QE2'S SEAGOING LIFE WAS ANNOUNCED AT 8AM ON MONDAY, 18TH JUNE 2007.

THAT WAS THE TIME CHOSEN BY CUNARD LINE, AND ITS AMERICAN PARENT COMPANY, TO TELL THE WORLD THAT ONE OF ITS BEST-LOVED ICONS WAS TO END HER DAYS AS A MIDDLE EASTERN HOTEL AT THE PALM JUMEIRAH IN DUBAI.

ON BOARD, OFF THE COAST OF NORWAY, CAPTAIN IAN MCNAUGHT HAD BRIEFED HIS OFFICERS AND CREW AS THE SHIP DEPARTED TRONDHEIM EN ROUTE TO AALESUND.

PASSENGERS ENJOYING THE 14-NIGHT VOYAGE OF THE VIKINGS CRUISE RECEIVED THE NEWS IN INDIVIDUAL LETTERS SIGNED BY CUNARD LINE PRESIDENT & MANAGING DIRECTOR CAROL MARLOW AND DELIVERED TO THEIR STATEROOMS.

She wrote:

"Dear Cunarder

QE2 TO LEAVE THE CUNARD FLEET IN NOVEMBER 2008

As you are a valued guest, I wanted to write personally to tell you that Queen Elizabeth 2, the most famous ship in the world, will be leaving the Cunard fleet in autumn 2008.

QE2 has sailed the world's seas for almost forty years, and has travelled over 5 million miles in the process; that is further than any other ship in history. She is the longest-serving ship in Cunard's 168-year history, and she has outlasted all other transatlantic liners.

After such an illustrious career, we feel that the time will be right for her to leave the fleet next year. However, she will not disappear. She has been purchased by Istithmar, the investment arm of Dubai World and a wholly owned company of the Government of Dubai.

She will be delivered to Dubai in November 2008, where she will cease her role as an ocean-going passenger vessel, and be refurbished and adapted to become a luxury floating hotel, retail and entertainment destination at The Palm Jumeirah.

We think it very important that QE2 should end her ocean going career with dignity. We are, therefore, very pleased to have secured a permanent home for her that will enable future generations to continue to experience fully both the ship and her history.

This is clearly going to be an emotional farewell. QE2 was launched by Her Majesty The Queen in September 1967, forty years ago this year, and since she came into service in 1969, she has carried over 2 million passengers, undertaken 25 World Cruises, and crossed the Atlantic over 800 times. And like many of her Cunard predecessors she has been a major attraction at ports around the world.

She will remain with the fleet until 11th November 2008, when she will leave her homeport of Southampton for the last time, to commence her final voyage to Dubai. We have reviewed her final season's sailings, and have made two itinerary changes, in order to celebrate the service of this magnificent ship and her historic departure in a fitting manner...

...Meanwhile, I hope you will be able to join us on one of our QE2 voyages, to celebrate the life of this wonderful ship.

Thank you again for your support of Cunard Line.

With kind regards,

Yours sincerely,

Carol Marlow
President & Managing Director